MAP OF AVEBURY AND SURROUNDING AREA

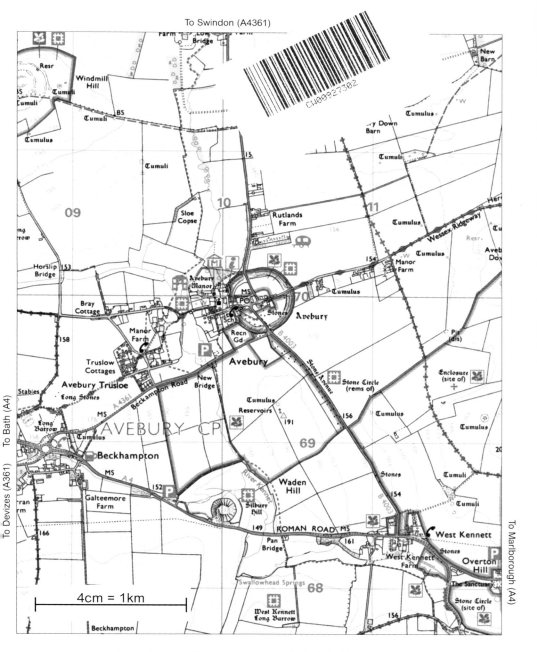

To Swindon (A4361)

To Devizes (A361) To Bath (A4)

To Marlborough (A4)

4cm = 1km

INTRODUCTION

Avebury is not Britain's best-known stone circle, but being 14 times the size of Stonehenge and predating it by around 500 years it is undoubtedly the greatest. Over the years a great deal of damage has been inflicted on the stones, some in the name of the Church and more when the ground was cleared for farming, but thankfully due to careful restoration in the 1930s there is still a lot to see as we walk freely amongst the stones.

Also, it does not stand in isolation but is the centre of a unique complex of prehistoric monuments all within a radius of 1½ miles (2½ km).

The site of the neolithic settlement at Windmill Hill can be located to the north-west of Avebury. Then to the south are the mysterious mound of Silbury Hill and the ancient burial tomb known as West Kennet Long Barrow. Another site that was once connected to Avebury by an avenue of stones is The Sanctuary which lies to the south-east.

The Stone Age people who built the circle and surrounding monuments around 5,000 years ago could not have just been concerned with their daily survival but must have had a culture that enabled them to produce these magnificent feats of engineering.

The village of Avebury surrounded by Britain's largest stone circle

At its prime the circular ditch at Avebury measured 9 metres (30ft) deep with four causewayed entrances roughly north, south, east and west. Inside the ditch 101 standing stones made up the enormous outer ring, and inside this were two smaller circles one with the Obelisk at its centre and the other a Cove. Outside the Obelisk circle stood a naturally perforated Ring Stone. And finally, there were stone processional avenues that led from each of the south and west gateways.

Over many years archaeologists have worked hard to discover the history of this impressive monument but there are many

questions that remain unanswered. New excavations and better technology mean that we are learning more all the time but it is unlikely that we will ever know for certain exactly why it was built.

However it was obviously an extremely important gathering place. Very little neolithic rubbish was found here so it is assumed that it was not the centre of a community but was more likely used for ritual purposes. It was perhaps a great temple for people who lived in close harmony with their natural environment, and ceremonies that related to the seasons and fertility are thought to have been practised here.

King Charles II was impressed enough by its description to visit Avebury in 1663.

Naturally occurring sarsen stones at Lockeridge Dene

BUILDING AVEBURY

The earliest architects of Avebury did not have the completed picture of stone circles, avenues and coves in their heads when they began. As with all old buildings it evolved over a long period of time with new generations modifying and making additions to suit their changing needs.

The henge was started around 3000 BC when the circular ditch was marked out and digging began. They used basic tools of antlers and bone to loosen the chalk which was then loaded into wicker baskets and hauled up to form the bank.

Measuring approximately 1 mile (1½ km) in circumference it

A henge is the name of a roughly circular earthwork consisting of a ditch and bank.

has been estimated that 100 thousand cubic metres (4 million cubic feet) of chalk were moved in this way. Certainly it would have taken more than one generation to complete.

The outer ring of megaliths was not added until around 500 years later. These slabs of sarsen - a kind of toughened sandstone - were found like natural stepping-stones all over the landscape to the south and east of Avebury at that time. They can still be seen at Lockeridge Dene near Marlborough where the original landscape has been preserved.

Suitable stones were laboriously dragged to the site on wooden sledges over the other stones and hills. Imagine the panic if one of the ropes had snapped under the stress and the men had to dive out of the way of a tumbling sarsen.

When they finally arrived at the site their work had only just begun. Each stone, weighing between 10 and 100 tonnes, was hoisted upright into a specially dug hole, inch by inch, with wooden levers and straining ropes. Once up, chalk was packed around the base to make it secure. It may have taken up to a year to shift and erect one of the larger stones.

The sarsens were not shaped but were chosen for their natural form and fall into one of two categories. Some are tall, rectangular pillars and these are thought to represent the male, while others are roughly diamond shaped symbolising the female

aspect. The stones also varied in size with the largest being used for the more important features. The gateway stones for instance are considerably larger than most others. Quite humbling for those who entered through them.

Inside this grand outer circle were two important features. The Obelisk was the largest of all the Avebury giants measuring nearly 7 metres (21ft) tall and towered a full 2 metres (7ft) higher than any other. Surrounded by a circle of 29 large diamond stones this colossal phallic symbol must have needed the strength of hundreds to raise it into its upright position.

The Cove on the other hand was made up of three huge female stones at right angles to each other with the open side facing

A 'female' diamond and a 'male' pillar standing opposite each other in West Kennet Avenue

northeast. This too was enclosed by another smaller circle of 27 stones and was sited slightly north of the Obelisk. Archaeologists discovered the beginnings of a third circle near the northern entrance but it had been dismantled before it was completed to make way for the ditch. This suggests that the inner circles were in place or built around the same time as the henge. More evidence to support this view was uncovered during the 2003 excavation at the Cove, which is now thought to have been erected around 3000 BC.

Sometime after the megaliths were placed work started on deepening the ditch that, when finished, measured a full 9 metres (30 ft) deep. This in turn raised the bank to around 6 metres (18 ft).

Chalk from the bottom of the enlarged ditch was used to pack the base of the Ring Stone which

Sarsen's get their name from the Anglo-Saxon words 'sar' meaning troublesome and 'stan' meaning stone.

was raised outside the Obelisk circle. At other neolithic sites these ring stones have been connected with fertility rites and this could be the case here as well.

And finally, the avenues were built in short straight sections. The one leading from the south entrance eventually connected to The Sanctuary over $1^1/_2$ miles ($2^1/_2$ km) away on Overton Hill.

The generations of labour involved with erecting this one monument alone reflects the importance that it held for its people. But with the passing of time their rituals and the true purpose for the circles were eventually forgotten.

West Kennet Avenue

The Southern Gateway

AVEBURY'S
DESTRUCTION

The circles stood unused for over a thousand years. In fact when the Romans visited during their occupation between the 1st and 4th centuries they would have seen the circles overgrown but more or less in their complete state.

It was probably used as a defensive position during the Saxon invasion but by the 6th century the Saxons were making their homes within the circle. They named the henge Weala-dic meaning 'ditch of the Britons'.

> The circles would have been seen by the Romans in their entirety.

Their stone built church made an appearance in the 10th century but was significantly sited just outside the pagan temple.

Yet, by the late 13th century Christianity was becoming more powerful and it decided that pagan symbols would no longer be tolerated. It decreed that the stones should be torn down and destroyed.

But the inhabitants of Avebury may have feared the Devil's retribution because the stones were not destroyed, but were painstakingly lowered then buried in pits. The removal of stones in this way went on for some years and a felled stone may have been the highlight of an annual festival.

At one such occasion a terrible accident struck a travelling barber-surgeon who was helping to overthrow a stone. As the sarsen was about to fall he slipped and was crushed under its enormous weight. There was little point in trying to prise it off again and as a result he lay in a grave of his own making for more than 600 years.

This seemed to bring about the end of the stone burials. Perhaps it terrified the villagers into thinking that the Devil did have something to say about it after all.

Sometime later in the second half of the 17th century the stones began to be cleared to make way for farming. This time the stones were demolished and the broken stones used for building.

Sarsen is an incredibly hard stone so a special technique was used to break them up into useful pieces. First the stone was placed in pit filled with burning straw then when scorching hot dowsed with lines of cold water to crack it. A good bash with a sledgehammer would then shatter it into manageable building blocks. The evidence of these stones is all around in the houses and garden walls of the village. Notice how some of it has reddened from the fire and water process.

Avebury's sarsens used in building

'Adam' and 'Eve' are the only surviving stones of the Beckhampton Avenue

It was at the height of this destruction that the antiquarian William Stukeley came upon Avebury and realised that it was an important ancient site. Even so, the clearance continued despite his protests. He recorded what he saw in detailed sketches marking stones as they fell. Although the mighty Obelisk had already fallen before he arrived he was witness to its incredible size before it too was tackled by a sledgehammer and broken.

He also surveyed and drew the stones of the Beckhampton Avenue. Unfortunately only two stones of this avenue remain. Known as Adam and Eve they stand in a field near the roundabout.

The years of destruction had taken their toll on the monument. The remaining stones were very overgrown and obscured by derelict buildings and farm rubbish. Any visitor would have had trouble realising that there was a monument here at all.

Alexander Keiller, a keen archaeologist in his spare time, was appalled by the neglect and bought the site in the early 20th century and began to re-establish it as the greatest stone circle in Britain.

From the 17th century stones were broken up using fire and water and used for building.

WILLIAM STUKELEY

William Stukeley was a doctor and a clergyman who was interested in British antiquity. After learning about Avebury from John Aubrey's writings he decided to visit and eventually spent five years meticulously recording and studying what he found.

He arrived in the village in 1719 when the population was growing rapidly and the stone breaking was at its most destructive. He could not prevent what was happening and mourned the loss of each stone. He resolved to draw it all before it completely disappeared.

In his search for detail he learned a great deal about the stones observing that the largest stones were used for gateways and other important focal points. Also he was the first to notice that the stones had a rough and a smooth side and that the 'better' smooth side always faced inwards.

Previously it was thought that these carefully laid out stones had been of Roman origin but Stukeley rightly supposed that they were much older than this. He began to speculate about who had erected them and why.

After getting so much right he then mistakenly attributed the building of Avebury to the druids - a discrepancy of around 2,000 years.

During his later years at Avebury he became obsessed with druidism and his drawings became distorted to fit in with his ideas. His contemporaries no longer took him seriously and consequently his work was disregarded by historians for a long time.

More recently though his drawings have helped archaeologists to visualise and understand Avebury's history. Alexander Keiller, the archaeologist who in the 1930s reconstructed some of the circle, was in possession of his earlier sketches and writings and used them successfully to discover missing stones.

They have also proved invaluable to more modern

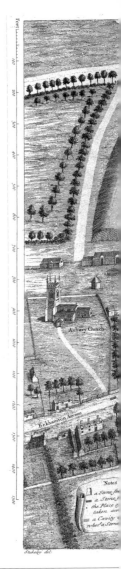

William Stukeley's 'great stone serpent'

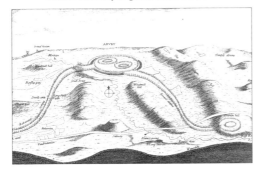

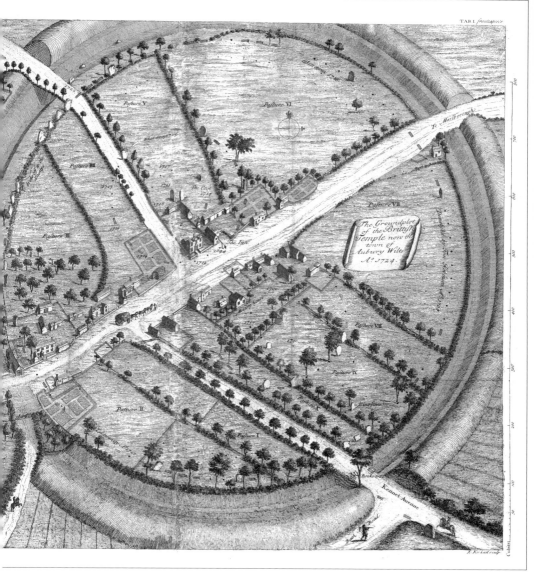

William Stukeley's ground plot of Avebury 1724

archaeologists in locating features such as the Beckhampton Avenue. This was thought to have only existed in Stukeley's imagination as the tail of his 'great stone serpent' but recent excavations have proved it to have been a

reality although it was not as stylised as the picture opposite shows.

Before William Stukeley came to Avebury, the circles were thought to have been built by the Romans.

ALEXANDER KEILLER

Alexander Keiller is regarded by some as Avebury's saviour.

Born in 1889 in Dundee, he became a pioneering archaeologist who cared passionately about the fate of Avebury. His extensive work carried out during the 1930s was entirely funded from his personal fortune inherited from his family's marmalade business.

Before Keiller came to Avebury the place was barely recognisable and was littered with derelict buildings and farm rubbish. His dream was to clear the circles of clutter and return them to their original splendour.

Alexander Keiller spent the equivalent of £2 million of his own money on Avebury.

He eventually bought the circle and most of the village and moved from London into Avebury Manor.

Local labourers were employed to help clear the debris and uncover the buried stones some of which were over a metre below the surface. The original stone holes were located and the megaliths were returned to them and securely cemented in.

His work became controversial when the villagers learned the full extent of his plan. They were glad of the work he

Stones found and re-erected by Keiller

provided in times when jobs were scarce, but the proposal to demolish their homes and relocate the inhabitants to brand new houses at Avebury Trusloe did not meet with everyone's approval. One villager recorded that two thirds of the village was torn down before he stopped.

His excavations included a third of the West Kennet Avenue and the western half of the outer circle. In the south-east quarter his attention concentrated on the inner circle but a diminishing fortune coupled with the onset of war meant it was never completed leaving many questions unanswered.

Yet his work has left us with a

Avebury Manor

magnificent monument that would almost certainly have disintegrated into obscurity had it not been for his tireless dedication.

Before he died in 1955 he sold Avebury to the National Trust. They offered £12,000, which he agreed to because he knew that Avebury would be in safe hands. But this sum only represented the agricultural value of the land, and was a fraction of the £50,000 he had invested in it (equivalent to an excess of £2 million today).

The Alexander Keiller Museum was founded by him in 1938 and is home to his finds from his Windmill Hill and Avebury excavations. Now also maintained by the National Trust it is located in the old stables near his former home.

Apart from archaeology
Keiller's passions included
skiing, fast cars and women.

13

The South-West Quarter

WALKING TOUR OF THE CIRCLE

Approximately 1mile (1$\frac{1}{2}$ km)

The Blacksmith's Stone

South-West Quarter

Begin at the gate to the side of the Henge Shop. This graceful arc of stones is one of the most complete sections of the circle and was restored by Alexander Keiller in the 1930s. Faced with an overgrown ruin he painstakingly located the stones that had been buried in medieval times to appease the Church and re-erected them into their original sockets. He used concrete markers to indicate stones that could not be found. These missing stones were probably cleared for farming and used for building in the village.

    The first stone inside the gate is a scarred survivor of that period. Now incomplete it was once a magnificent giant and one of a pair that guarded the west entrance to the circle. The remaining fragments of this stone were recovered from the old blacksmiths forge and were glued and bolted together again before being returned to its former position. If you look closely you can still see the blacksmith's iron wedge used to try and split the stone jammed near the base.

The sixth remaining stone in the arc is known as the Barber's Stone and was the site of a terrible accident. For while this stone was being toppled into a large hole one of the workers was crushed beneath it as it fell. Little did he know that when he was helping to dig the hole he was actually digging his own grave. The stone was too heavy to lift again and as the man was certainly dead it was left where it was and buried. It was

The concrete markers show where a stone once stood.

Avebury was a striking white monument in a fertile green landscape for many years before the grass took hold of the chalk.

not until around 600 years later when the stone was raised again that his skeleton was discovered and with it were a pair of scissors, an iron probe and three silver coins. These items indicated that he was probably a travelling barber-surgeon and ever since this unfortunate soul has been known by this name.

Further round you will notice where the bank has been levelled. This is not an original feature but where road builders dug into it for earth to raise the road.

After exploring the rest of this section use the gate to cross the busy road and enter the south-east quarter.

The Barber's Stone

South-East Quarter

At first it may be difficult to make sense of this jumble of stones. This is because it was only partially excavated by Keiller before his work was interrupted by wartime activities. It was recently discovered that there are still many stones lying beneath the turf.

The arc of five large stones joined by four concrete markers are the remains of the 29 stones of the southern inner circle. At the centre is a large fluted marker that shows us where the imposing Obelisk once stood flanked by the smaller, mysterious 'Z' Stones. This supposed phallic symbol was recorded by William Stukeley as towering over two metres (7ft) taller than any other stone at Avebury.

Walk parallel to the road

towards the bank and to the two impressive stones that are the south gateway. The stone on your right is known as the Devil's Chair the reason why will become apparent as you turn and look at it from the other side. The natural seat in this stone has been a rest stop for countless visitors and many have had their photo taken here. But take care as you sit because if it is raining the water funnels down from above onto your head. This 'chimney', according to local legend, has also been known to smoke. In another story, the Devil can be summoned by running around the stone 100 times in an anti-clockwise

The Devil's Chair

The 'Z' Stones

direction. Presumably these devil stories grew up to dissuade God fearing Christians from visiting the pagan stones.

Climb up onto the bank and view the scene from above. The pattern becomes a little clearer from this position and you can also see the broken stump of the fallen Ring Stone.

Turn and look behind you to see West Kennet Avenue disappearing over the low hill. These pairs of stones once stretched for $1\frac{1}{2}$ miles ($2\frac{1}{2}$ km) to the Sanctuary on Overton Hill, and were used as a processional way to, or possibly from, the circle. The part you can see was Keiller's initial project at Avebury. He resurrected a third of the avenue and discovered a pattern of opposing stone shapes with each pair he reinstated. There is a gate to cross the road and explore the avenue if you wish.

Rejoin the circle and walk all the way around the bank until you reach the two fallen megaliths under the trees noticing as you do the ridges that were field boundaries in Stukeley's time. At the end of the bank is the gate to gain access into the next quarter.

Stories of the Devil grew up around the stones to deter Christians from the pagan circles.

Stukeley's view of the Cove 1723

Abury

North-East Quarter

The road you have just crossed was the circle's main entrance for travellers and traders in neolithic times and still leads up to the ancient Ridgeway Path on top of the hill. The Ridgeway was an important route and its proximity to Avebury is probably significant.

Today, to come from the Ridgeway on foot down this quiet lane is still one of the most pleasant ways to enter the circle.

Once across the lane you are now in the north-east quarter.

The first fallen giant on your left was a gateway stone and one of the very few remaining megaliths in this sector. This is the one area of the circle that has not been excavated and you can see what a thorough a job the religious zealots and farmers did. But a survey carried out by the National Trust in 2003 on the eastern half of the circle has confirmed what many had previously believed; as many as 15 stones remain buried here. The survey clearly defined the size and shape of the megaliths and their original positions but at present there are no plans to re-erect them.

If you look closely at the inner side of the bank you may be able to see the shelf that stopped soil falling from the top of the bank into the ditch below. This feature is know as a berm and is particularly clear in this part of the circle.

Travellers and traders would have used the eastern gateway as the main entrance into the circle.

Behind the buildings are two large stones standing at right angles to each other. This Cove was once made up of three proud sarsens standing in a U-shape. The open side faced north-east and may have been roughly aligned with the most northerly moonrise. The two remaining stones have recently been straightened and set in lime concrete because there was some concern about their safety. During the work archaeologists were surprised to find that the stones were much bigger than previously thought.

The Cove's open side faced north-east towards the moon's most northerly rising point.

As many as 15 megaliths lie buried in the eastern half of the circle.

Once estimated at 50 tonnes they are now supposed to weigh around twice that.

The Cove was surrounded by the northern inner circle, which had a diameter of approximately 98 metres (320 ft) and consisted of 27 stones.

Where the 'Z' Stones flanked the Obelisk so a second smaller circle once skirted the Cove. If we consider that the Obelisk circle represents the male gender then this must surely be the opposing female circle.

There is a gate near The Cove to exit this quarter.

The North-East Quarter

North-West Quarter

The most striking stone in this area is the Diamond or Swindon Stone that balances precariously on one of its corners and overhangs the road. People, especially children, can often be seen giving it a wide birth to avoid walking under it just in case it should suddenly fall. It is one of the north gateway stones and it also has mysterious stories associated with it.

Local legend will have you believe that it crosses the road at midnight in search of its missing partner. Another tale tells that, again at the stroke of midnight, it spins through 360° on its axis. But in fact this stone has not moved for around 4,500 years, and as one of the few to remain standing in its

The Diamond Stone is said to cross the road at midnight to look for its lost partner.

original position it is unlikely to do so now.

Near to the Diamond Stone are three of Keiller's concrete markers. They show the position of what is thought to be the beginnings of a third small circle that was started before the ditch was dug. It was never finished and was dismantled long before the Diamond Stone was erected. This supports the evidence that the inner circles are older than earthwork.

Nine stones of the Cove's circle would have been in this quarter and The Red Lion now covers the position of some of them.

The Diamond or Swindon Stone

The North-West Quarter

The beginnings of another small circle were found here and predates the ditch and the bank.

This was the first quarter that Keiller restored and he discovered eight buried stones some over a metre (4 ft) below the surface. He returned them to their sockets and set about clearing the overgrown areas sometimes resorting to controlled explosions to remove stubborn roots.

One part he did not rectify was the bank, which was cut into to make room for the Great Barn. The Lord of the Manor, who had little regard for the old earthwork, did this in the 17th century.

When you come to the end of this final section and descend the steps notice how the ditch continues round behind The Granary (now The National Trust Shop) and into the gardens beyond. The stone circle stops much shorter due to the buildings. No doubt Keiller had planned to pull these down to get to the stones beneath. The National Trust now has a policy of retaining the houses as part of Avebury's history and has no intention of removing any more.

From here you can turn left to return to the High Street, or right to explore the Alexander Keiller Museum, The Great Barn, St James' Church and perhaps visit the Café.

Some of the Cove circle stones would have been in the north-west quarter.

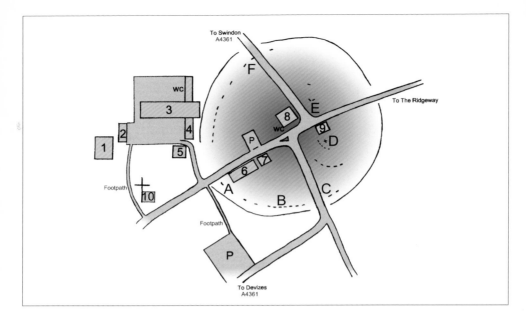

THE STONES

A - The Blacksmith's Stone
B - The Barber's Stone
C - The Devil's Chair
D - Position of the Obelisk
E - The Cove
F - The Diamond or Swindon Stone

AVEBURY VILLAGE

1 - The Manor
Avebury Manor was built during the reign of Queen Elizabeth I on the site of a 12th century Benedictine priory and has been added to and updated over the years. The grounds are particularly attractive with interesting topiary and several walled gardens. Watch out for the hooded monk who is said to haunt the grounds.

Opening hours are limited so please check to avoid disappointment.

2 - Alexander Keiller Museum
This National Trust museum is situated in the stable block near to the Manor entrance. Founded in 1938 by Keiller himself it is home to his collection of finds and provides a fascinating insight into the archaeology of Avebury and surrounding monuments.

3 - The Great Barn
Part of the henge bank was levelled in the 17th century to build this thatched threshing barn. The large doors at either end were to enable a horse and full wagon to enter at one end, unload, and leave through the other without having the inconvenience of turning around.

Inside it now is the National Trust exhibition 'Avebury 6000 Years of Mystery'.

The Dovecote

The small circular building with no windows is a dovecote. The birds enter through the opening in the roof and inside nest in one of the hundreds of holes that line its walls. It belonged to the Manor, and the birds were used as a source of fresh meat for the Lord during the winter months.

The Dovecote

4 - The Circle Café

In the old stable block adjacent to the barn is the National Trust café. They open for coffee, lunches and afternoon teas.

5 - National Trust Shop

Housed in the old Granary near to the cafe is the shop that sells the Trust's range of quality gifts.

6 - The Henge Shop

Next to the post office is the Henge Shop. An excellent place for quality gifts, cards and guides. It also has an interesting book section including an extensive range of archaeological publications.

7 - The Post Office and Shop

The local village store that sells stamps, groceries, snacks and drinks.

The Henge Shop

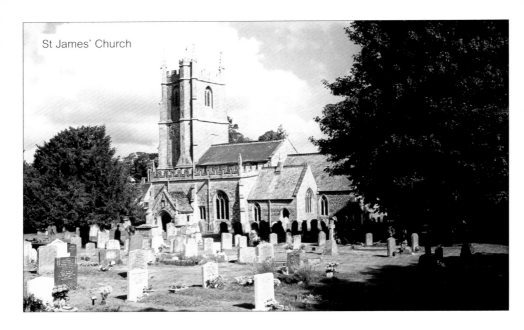
St James' Church

8 - The Red Lion

The public house is situated on the the cross roads at the centre of the stone circle. At night a ghostly horse drawn coach has been known to clatter across its cobbled forecourt. During the day though it is an ideal place to sit and enjoy a drink when the weather is fine. Inside you may encounter Florrie, a 300 year old ghost, who was thrown down the well by her husband when he discovered she had been unfaithful. The well is still a feature in the pub but is now rather wisely covered with glass.

9 - Tourist Information Centre

The Chapel on Green Street was built in the early 18th century from the circle's broken stones. It is the only Church building to have been raised inside the pagan circle.

Nowadays it is home to the Tourist Information Centre although church services are still held on some Sundays.

10 - St James' Church

The Church can be dated back to before the Norman Conquest (1066) and has been subjected to numerous additions and alterations. A particularly rare feature is the rood loft that survived the Reformation by being hidden behind plaster. It was not until 1810 that it was rediscovered and restored. The font is around a thousand years old and part of the original church although it was an unadorned stone tub at that time. The carving on it was not done until the around the 12th century.

WINDMILL HILL

The site is approximately 1¹/₂ miles (2¹/₂ km) north of Avebury and can be reached on foot by heading west down the High Street and then following the footpath until it reaches Bray Street. This leads to the track that takes you to Windmill Hill.

Alternatively by car, turn right out of the main car park and then take the next right to Avebury Trusloe. Continue to the end of the road and turn left into Bray Street where there is limited parking. Follow the track up the hill.

Windmill Hill was one of the largest and probably one of the most important causewayed enclosures in Britain. It was inhabited by early farmers and traders many years before Avebury was built. Situated on a low hill it covered an area of 8¹/₂ hectares (21 acres) and was an arrangement of

Seashells and 'foreign' pottery suggest that the people who lived here were traders.

three irregular rings of ditches. There is not much left to see today but at one time the outermost ditch was over 2 metres (7 ft) deep.

It came to Alexander Keiller's attention in 1924 and, after finding out that it was going to be developed, decided to buy it and investigate further.

He paid particular attention to the ditches where he found broken arrowheads, antler combs and whelk shells along with human skulls and long bones.

Other interesting finds included chalk phallic symbols leading us to believe that fertility rituals played an important part in the lives of the people who lived here.

An exhibition of these artefacts can be seen at the Keiller Museum in Avebury.

Windmill Hill

SILBURY HILL

Silbury Hill lies approximately 1 mile (1$\frac{1}{2}$ km) to the south of Avebury and can be reached on foot by the path opposite the main Avebury car park. Alternatively by road, turn right out of the car park. When you reach the roundabout take the first left and continue until you reach the Silbury car park and viewing area. The Hill is an English Heritage site and also a site of Special Scientific Interest, which means the climbing of the hill is strictly forbidden.

After two centuries of investigation the purpose for Silbury Hill still remains a mystery.

For a long time most people believed that it was a larger version of the round barrows used for burials that can be seen

For many years Silbury was thought to be a burial mound.

throughout the area. Over the years these burial mounds were plundered for their treasures. It was assumed that as Silbury was so large it was built for a very important person and so would contain treasure beyond most people's dreams. Perhaps Europe's equivalent of an Egyptian pyramid.

Legend says that buried in the mound were life-size figures of King Sil (or Zel) and his horse made of gold.

No wonder then that three tunnels have been dug into it. The first was in 1776 when the Duke of Northumberland and Colonel Drax

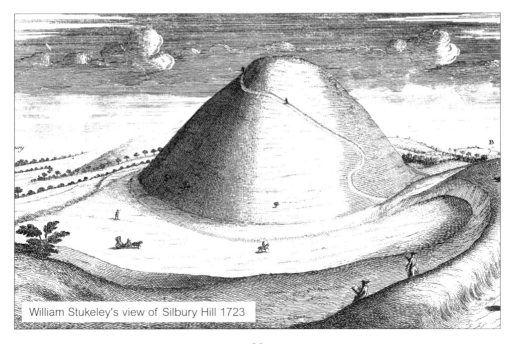

William Stukeley's view of Silbury Hill 1723

Silbury Hill

hired a team of miners to sink a shaft from the top of the hill. The next was led by Dean Merewether on behalf of the Archaeological Institute in 1849 who tunnelled in from the side. Lastly, in 1968, the BBC and Cardiff University sponsored another tunnel running close to the second. None of these discovered any treasure although the last did uncover important structural details and the remains of antler picks that were radio-carbon dated to around 2400 BC.

It was not simply a pile of chalk but a complex and well planned structure built by people with an understanding of soil mechanics. The chalk was built up in six circular layers, each one smaller than the last, with a web of reinforcement walls to keep things in place. This arrangement, and the sloping sides of 60 degrees,

meant that it was incredibly stable.

Despite this in 2000 it was in danger of collapsing when a large hole appeared in the top. It was discovered that the first tunnel had not been filled in properly. Fortunately now that structural work has been completed it is thought to be stable again.

As the largest man-made mound in Europe it covers an area just over 2 hectares ($5\frac{1}{2}$ acres) and stands 40 metres (130 ft) high. It would have taken 18 million man-hours to shift the 230,000 cubic metres (8 million cubic feet) of chalk to build it making it the most time consuming monument in the Avebury complex.

Winged ants were found under the hill suggesting that construction began in late summer.

The Long Barrow S. of Silbury Hill.

William Stukeley's view of West Kennet Long Barrow

WEST KENNET
LONG BARROW

It lies approximately 2 miles (3 km) south of Avebury and can be reached on foot by taking the footpath opposite the main car park to Silbury Hill . By car turn right out of the main car park and then at the roundabout turn left onto the A4. Silbury Hill's car park is on the left; you can either park here or, continue for $1/4$ mile ($1/2$ km) to the lay-by on the right. From there take the footpath over the water meadow and continue to top of the hill.

The long shape on the brow of the hill is one of the largest neolithic burial mounds in Britain. Originally it was surrounded on three sides by a ditch that was 3 metres (10 ft) deep and 6 metres (20 ft) wide.

At the front a semi-circular forecourt graced the entrance. Facing east, as it does, the early morning sun would have penetrated the barrow's gloomy interior.

The tomb's use spanned an enormous length of time, from maybe as early as 3500BC to 2000BC, when for some reason the chambers were filled with stones and soil and the entrance sealed with the large slabs of sarsen you see today.

When opened, the bones of numerous bodies were found in disarray. It is thought that corpses

The bones of around fifty bodies were found scattered on the floor.

were allowed to decompose in a mortuary house and significant bones removed before the rest were thrown into the tomb. This made it very difficult to calculate the exact number of bodies that were here. There were piles of vertebrae, heaps of long bones and some bones even poked into crevices, but mostly they just littered the floor.

In the first chamber on your right the only complete skeleton was found squatting in the corner. His death was almost certainly caused by the arrowhead embedded in his neck.

The stone passageway and chambers are the only parts of the tomb that have been made accessible and occupies about a

A row of skulls was found in the second chamber on your left.

A local doctor used the bones he found in the barrow to make a medicine for his unsuspecting patients.

sixth of the 104 metre (340 ft) barrow. It is supposed that the remaining part was constructed with wooden chambers but as yet has not been investigated.

Although, in the late 1600's Dr Toope, nicknamed Dr Took, regularly dug into the side of the mound and caused considerable damage to the barrow. He had found a good supply of human bones to make, as he put it, 'a noble medicine that relieved many of my distressed neighbours.'

Interestingly, many of the bones showed cases of spina bifida and nearly all the adults had signs of arthritis.

Sarsen slabs that sealed the tomb

THE SANCTUARY

Turn left out of Avebury's main car park. Then take the first right onto the B4003 and follow the avenue to the T-junction. Turn left onto the A4 and The Sanctuary is on the right hand side of the road opposite the Ridgeway Path.

The Sanctuary today seems less impressive than Avebury's stone circles and Silbury Hill's great mass. In 1668 it was mentioned in Samuel Pepys' diary where he likened it to the building at Stonehenge. But now nothing is left of the original structure and its existence is only marked by concrete bricks arranged in seven concentric circles.

The largest and third largest circles were constructed of sarsen stones that stood about $1\frac{1}{2}$ metres (5 ft) high while the others were

The Sanctuary was probably used as a mortuary house.

made from wooden posts. It is uncertain whether these posts were freestanding or were part of the walls of a thatched hut.

It was however an important part of the Avebury complex as it was connected by West Kennet Avenue. William Stukeley thought it was the head of his 'great stone serpent' but it was perhaps more useful than his fanciful representation. Due to the large amount of human remains found here its purpose was likely a mortuary house. The dead would have been taken here to rot before some of the bones were interred in one of the barrows. Many of the bones found in West Kennet Long Barrow were scorched and it is possible that this took place at the Sanctuary to hasten decay.

Prospect of the Temple on Overton Hill. 8 July 1723.

TAB. XXI
P. 40

William Stukeley's view of the Sanctuary before the stones were removed 1723

Stukeley d.   The Hakpen, or head of the Snake, in ruins.